Strategic Planning
FOR ACTIVITIES & SPORTS PROGRAMMES IN INTERNATIONAL SCHOOLS

ERLEND BADHAM

Copyright © 2021 Erlend Badham

All rights reserved.

ISBN: 9798590123148

DEDICATION

To Dione,
The half of me who has made me whole since we met.

CONTENTS

	Acknowledgments	i
1	Who Should Use This Booklet?	Pg 1
2	The Roadmap to Strategic Planning	Pg 3
3	Preparation	Pg 6
4	Creating an ASP Vision	Pg 13
5	Discover Present State	Pg 21
6	SWOT Analysis	Pg 29
7	Define Focus Areas	Pg 33
8	Strategic Goals and Projects	Pg 36
9	Monitor Progress	Pg 42
10	Summary	Pg 45

References	Pg 48
Got Feedback?	Pg 50
About the Author	Pg 51

ACKNOWLEDGMENTS

Illustrations are designed by pch.vector / Freepik

1 WHO SHOULD USE THIS BOOKLET?

STRATEGIC PLANNING

This booklet is for Directors of Activities and Sport working in International Schools, and people aspiring for these roles. It takes the current "best practices" within strategic planning for businesses and applies it to the needs of typical Activities and Sports Programmes (ASP).

If you are responsible for the setting up and running of ASPs, then this booklet will help you understand the key components and structure of a strategic plan within this domain.

By following the steps outlined in this booklet, you will be able to understand the critical components of a strategy, how to approach setting and developing a strategy and some of the strategic tools to use. A clear strategic plan will inspire your staff, your management and your community and help build a positive culture around your programme.

2 THE ROADMAP TO STRATEGIC PLANNING

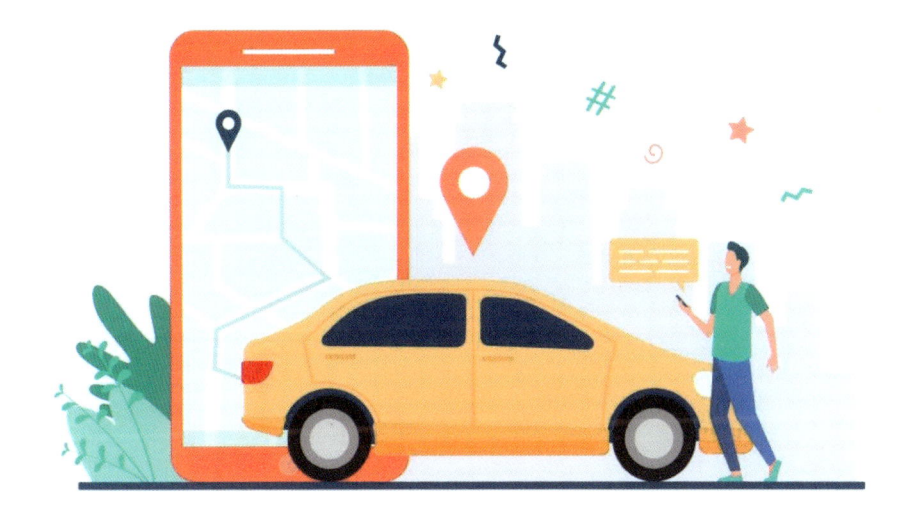

STRATEGIC PLANNING

Strategy has been defined as a general plan to achieve one or more long-term goals under conditions of uncertainty (Wikipedia, 2020).

Once created, your strategy includes actionable items and measurements that ensure your movement towards your long-term goals. Following is a mindmap of the process this booklet details. It gives an excellent conceptional overview which can be used as a reference point as you work through your strategic planning.

The ASP Roadmap

The ASP Roadmap

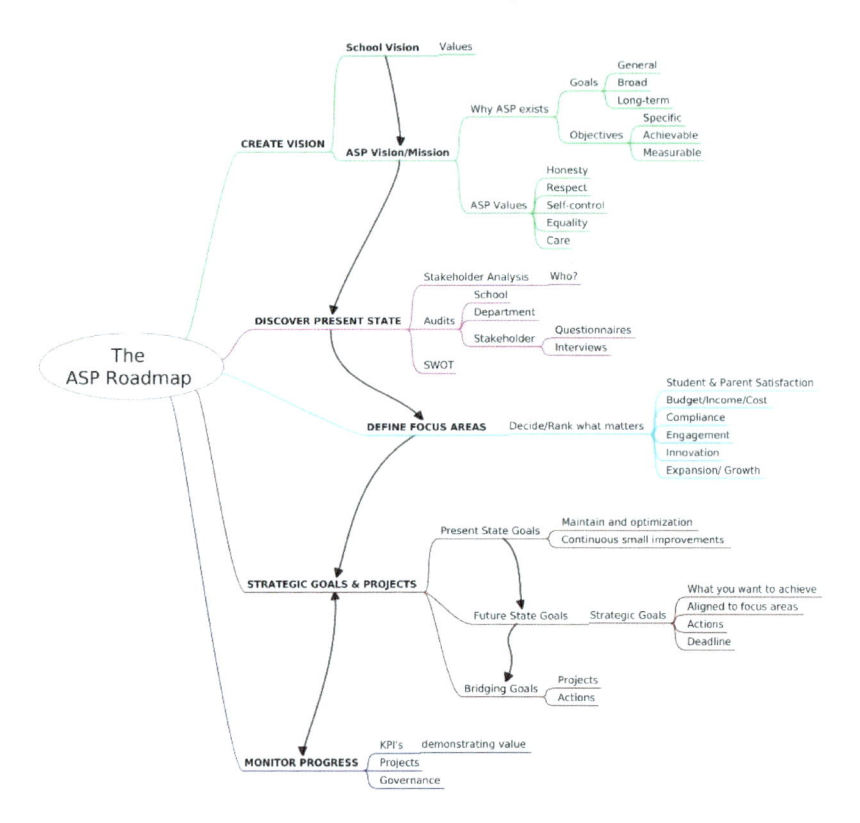

- **CREATE VISION**
  - School Vision
  - Values
  - ASP Vision/Mission
    - Why ASP exists
      - Goals
        - General
        - Broad
        - Long-term
      - Objectives
        - Specific
        - Achievable
        - Measurable
    - ASP Values
      - Honesty
      - Respect
      - Self-control
      - Equality
      - Care

- **DISCOVER PRESENT STATE**
  - Stakeholder Analysis — Who?
  - Audits
    - School
    - Department
    - Stakeholder
      - Questionnaires
      - Interviews
  - SWOT

- **DEFINE FOCUS AREAS** — Decide/Rank what matters
  - Student & Parent Satisfaction
  - Budget/Income/Cost
  - Compliance
  - Engagement
  - Innovation
  - Expansion/Growth

- **STRATEGIC GOALS & PROJECTS**
  - Present State Goals
    - Maintain and optimization
    - Continuous small improvements
  - Future State Goals — Strategic Goals
    - What you want to achieve
    - Aligned to focus areas
    - Actions
    - Deadline
  - Bridging Goals
    - Projects
    - Actions

- **MONITOR PROGRESS**
  - KPI's — demonstrating value
  - Projects
  - Governance

STRATEGIC PLANNING

Having a well-developed programme strategy will give you and your staff a sense of clarity and purpose that gives confidence to the school community. You will be aware of where you are going and how to get there. You will know whether you are on track or not, and be able to make adjustments as you go as well as justify why you are prioritising one area over another.

According to Lamothe, these are some of the benefits of having a strategy in place:

- *Provides a framework for goal setting and decision-making;*
- *Provides an opportunity for people to contribute their ideas and have input in the decision-making process;*
- *Provides a basis for measuring performance;*
- *Allows the stakeholders to ask and answer key questions;*
- *Clarifies opportunities and threats leading to better decisions;*
- *Challenges the status quo;*
- *Helps to drive innovation throughout the organisation.*

(Lamothe, 2013)

3 PREPARATION

Acquire Key Knowledge

When planning where to take your ASP, it is essential to be up to date on the current movements and research within this domain. The following search words are useful to get you started on finding relevant research:
- Literature review (extracurricular activities/sports programmes)
- Framework for planning youth sport programmes
- Erikson's stages of psychosocial development
- Youth development
- Physical literacy

I Below are a few relevant bullet points on the benefits of ASP:
- Mahoney (Mahoney, 2000) found that participation in voluntary, school-based, extracurricular activity increases students participation and achievement in school, facilitating:
    - Interpersonal skills
    - Positive social norms
    - Membership in prosocial peer groups
    - Stronger emotional and social connections to one's school
- Eccles et al. (Eccles et al., 2003) found that participation in extracurricular activities provided opportunities for students:
    - To acquire and practice social, physical and intellectual skills.
    - To contribute to one's community and develop a sense of agency.
    - Belong to a recognised social group that is valued in the community
    - To establish social networks with peers and adults that can help in crises.
    - To experience and deal with the challenges of everyday adolescent life.

Erikson developed the theory of psychosocial development. He believes that personality develops in stages. In each stage, Erikson believes people experience a conflict that serves as a turning point in their development. If people successfully deal with the conflict, they emerge from the stage with psychological strengths that will serve them well for the rest of their lives. If they fail to deal effectively with these conflicts, they may not develop the essential skills needed for a strong sense of self.

As ASPs' roles in international schools are often the holistic development of students, Erikson's theory is relevant. It allows us to plan for the psychosocial stages and conflicts to develop the students in our care best.

On the next page are the stages of psychosocial development relevant for ASP planning:

Relevant Stages from Eriksons Psychosocial Development Stages

Stage	Basic Conflict	Important Events	Key Questions to be answered	Outcome
Preschool (3 to 5)	Initiative vs. Guilt	Exploration/ Play	Am I good or bad?	Children need to begin asserting control and power over the environment. Success in this state leads to a sense of purpose. Children who try to exert too much power experience disapproval, resulting in a sense of guilt.
School Age (6 to 11)	Industry vs. Inferiority	School/ Activities	How can I be good?	Children need to cope with new social and academic demands. Success leads to a sense of competence, while failure results in feeling of inferiority.
Adolescence (12 to 18)	Identity vs. Role Confusion	Social Relationships/ Identity	Who am I and where am I going?	Teens need to develop a sense of self and personal identity. Success leads to an ability to stay true to yourself, while failure leads to role confusion and a weak sense of self.

From the research, we can infer the following points as being beneficial elements in an ASP:

- **Freedom of choice** - students engage in a desired activity
- **Learning environment** - the activity is set within an environment promoting initiative, surrounded by caring adult mentors and a positive group or community with opportunities for students to be important individuals.
- **Focus on life skills** - students learn and acquire life skills relevant to their psychosocial development stage.

Freedom of Choice

"Based on an examination of the best practices identified by youth development experts, psychosocial growth is most likely to occur when young people are engaged in a desired activity within an appropriate environment..." (Petitpas et al., 2005, p. 66)

Freely chosen activities provide the internal motivation to push oneself persistently.

Learning Environment

Following are some of the critical elements needed to create a positive learning environment within ASPs.

The ASP environment should develop a sense of initiative in young people. In an environment that develops initiative, individuals engage because they find the activity intrinsically motivating, challenging and important enough to put in time and effort (Csikszentmihalyi et al., 1993). Further attributes such as creativity, leadership, altruism and civic engagement are also linked with a student's initiative (Larson, 2000).

Erickson established that the critical events in the psychosocial development of teens focus on social relationships and identity. Participation in ASPs provides students with an ideal opportunity to develop relationships and their identity in their social world. Further opportunities for students to give back to the community also helps their sense of value and identity (Petitpas et al., 2005) and can be linked to leadership development.

The quality of adult relationships, behaviour and expectations of students, help frame the ASP environment for students. Coaches and leaders are effective when they are involved and hold high and positive expectations of their students. Parents are often in the best position to reinforce appropriate behaviours and attitudes taught by ASPs. Finding positive ways to include parents in your programme is well worth the effort.

Focus on Life Skills

It is beneficial for the ASP to focus on systematically teaching life skills and have strategies to promote the transfer of these skills to other domains within the school so that students can internalise them. For example, ASP activities that include goal-setting, self-appraisal and future planning are likely to help students in developing a clear identity with ambitions (Catalano et al., 2004). Having the same life skills taught in different activities helps with the transferability.

Through sports and activities, the coaches and leaders can be teaching a broad range of social, planning and problem-solving competencies. These competencies should be incorporated into the activity rather than taught as a separate topic. For example, require students to plan their schedule during a football tournament, ensuring they get to matches on time. Progressively students will internalise such skills as their typical approach to life situations.

ASP Benefits List

Creating a list of benefits is essential for understanding and conveying what value your programme offers to your significant stakeholders (students, parents, staff etc.). It is also useful for understanding why your ASP exists in the first place. Think about what your programme offers students and the school that the regular curriculum is less effective at?

As you work through your strategic planning, you will continuously refer to and update the benefits list.

As a focus group, brainstorm what the programme benefits are. The following is an example of what the result of your brainstorm might look like.

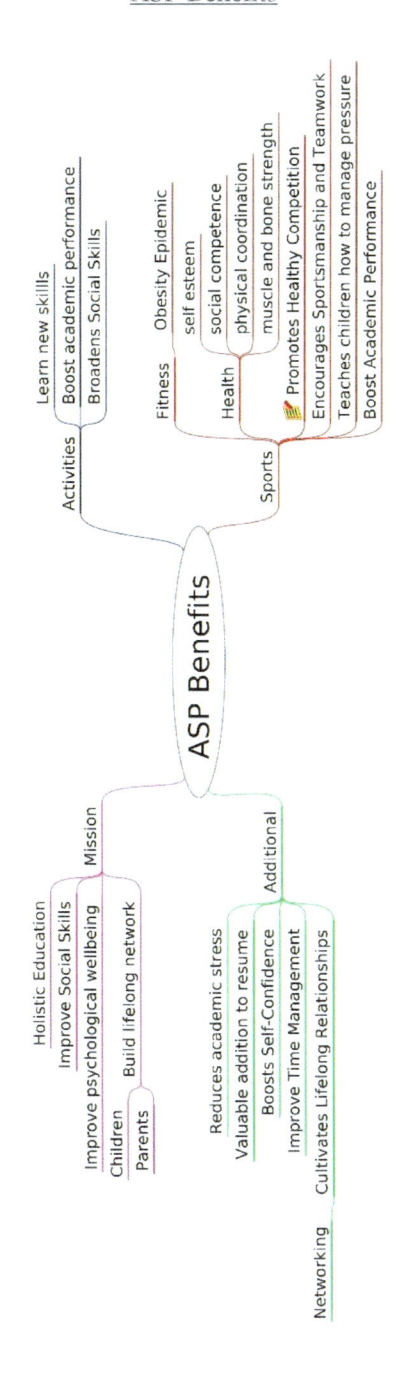

STRATEGIC PLANNING

ASP Benefits

ASP Benefits

- Activities
  - Learn new skills
  - Boost academic performance
  - Broadens Social Skills
- Sports
  - Fitness
    - Obesity Epidemic
    - self esteem
    - social competence
    - physical coordination
    - muscle and bone strength
  - Health
  - Promotes Healthy Competition
  - Encourages Sportsmanship and Teamwork
  - Teaches children how to manage pressure
  - Boost Academic Performance
- Mission
  - Holistic Education
  - Improve Social Skills
  - Improve psychological wellbeing
  - Build lifelong network
  - Children
  - Parents
- Additional
  - Reduces academic stress
  - Valuable addition to resume
  - Boosts Self-Confidence
  - Improve Time Management
- Networking
  - Cultivates Lifelong Relationships

Gain Support and Build a Work Group

As you are deciding on the direction of your programme and since the programme is a significant part of the school, the Director's and the school leadership's support is essential. The development of the ASP must be part of the school's evolutionary process. The Director must be kept up to date (if not directly involved) on what the ASP vision and requirements are, and be prepared to help by taking executive action.

Involve key team members in your strategic planning. Two (or more) heads with differing perspectives are better than one. Equally important is fostering "buy-in". Having helped create the strategy, this small group will be motivated to secure a broader engagement within the school and community for your strategic objectives and projects.

Identify highly experienced representatives from Marketing, Finance & Administration, Information Technology, Human Resources, Teaching Staff and the ASP Department Staff.

By selecting the core strategic planning team from a range of positions in your school and programme, you are more likely to achieve a balanced view of each planning aspect.

There are many ways of involving people. It could be focus groups, individual meetings with questionnaires, surveys or sending out updates and asking for open and honest feedback. It does not all have to be group meetings.

4 CREATING AN ASP VISION

When creating the ASP Vision Statement, remember that it must support and contribute to the school's overall vision statement. It should describe what the ASP programme (ideally) will be in 5 to 10 years and also its value. It should focus your strategy on what matters most and empower your staff in their execution of the ASP Strategy Plan. It should be simple, easily understood and provide unity of purpose.

School Vision

Gather information on the school's vision and strategic plan. Ask yourself:

- "What is the school's Vision Statement?"
- "What is the school's strategic plan?"
- "What are the specific characteristics of the parents and students we are catering for?"
- "Who are our main competitors?"

Find relevant information. Use it to align your strategy with the school's overall strategy, ensuring that you are moving in the right direction.

Breaking down the whole school vision statement will help you refine what role the ASP should take to help fulfil it. Look at the keywords used in the vision statement and uncover how your ASP can contribute.

Let's take the vision statement of the International School of Lausanne (ISL) as an example:

"ISL will be a world leader in international education. We will be acknowledged for our genuine care for the well-being of all members of our community, and for providing a challenging, innovative, holistic, values-based education that develops in young people the knowledge, skills and disposition to bring about positive change." ('About Us | International School of Lausanne, Switzerland', 2020)

There are several key concepts in their statement we could draw upon to make an underlying ASP vision:

- *World leader in international education* - being a world leader means quality, service and value. Are these aspects that should be highlighted in your programme?
- *Genuine care for well-being* - should your programme focus on community, health and happiness?
- *Providing a challenging, innovative, holistic, values-based education* - what

could the ASA and Sports Programme provide in terms of these factors? Innovative, suggests new and contemporary activities or methods. Values-based indicates a focus on standards, beliefs and ideals. Holistic means developing every aspect of the human (intellectual, social, emotional, physical and spiritual)

- *Develops in young people the knowledge, skills and disposition to bring about positive change* - should your focus be on gaining knowledge, skills and ambitions in certain areas?

Vision Statement Creation

With your focus group, brainstorm the questions:

- What purpose does the Activities and Sports Programme serve in the school setting?
- What do we want to accomplish?

When developing your answers to each question, consider how the question relates to the following stakeholders:

- Students
- Parents
- School

Once you have completed a brainstorm on these questions, ask your team to write out their answers (there can be more than one answer per question) on post-it notes. Stick the answers on a board, then start grouping similar answers together. This should give you an indication of where you as a group, feel your programme has more value and relevance.

Based on where you feel your programme brings the most value and relevance, formulate what that value could be in 5 - 10 years from now. Remember to make your vision statement short and memorable.

Here is a fictional example of an ASP vision based on the ISL example mentioned earlier, where the focus is on well-being and value-based education.

To foster joy, confidence and community through our ASP by placing the highest value on integrity and character.

Here are a few other examples from business and schools as well as fictional ones:

- "*Bring inspiration and innovation to every athlete in the world*" (Nike, 2020)
- "*…to put Christian principles into practice through programs that build healthy spirit, mind and body for all…*" (YMCA, 2020)
- Sport for all
- Provide students opportunities for holistic growth through co-curricular experiences.

- Be a force for youth development through values and innovation.

Writing your vision is a difficult task, and it takes time. After arriving at your first vision statement, it is a good idea to take some time away and come back to work with a fresh mind. You might see things in a slightly different light then and want to make some corrections.

Core Values

"Your personal core values define who you are, and a company's core values ultimately define the company's character and brand. For individuals, character is destiny. For organisations, culture is destiny." Tony Hsieh

Values are a significant contributor to what your programme's culture will be. They are your standards, beliefs, and ideals that will be shared within your staff and students and provide guidance to what is good or bad, desirable, or undesirable. They represent the essence of your programme's code of conduct, and they should answer the questions:

- What are our core beliefs?
- What principles guide us?

Most schools already have a set of values. Your job then is to look at how the school's values influence your programme and more importantly, the culture you are fostering.

Values are not words that sound good in a glossy marketing brochure but have little relevance elsewhere. They are supposed to be applied pragmatically.

For example, if the school's values include respect, then you need to set things up so that you are actively rewarding students when they apply that value. The use of reinforcement in sports, for example, is an effective way of highlighting the athletes' application of respect for each other and others on the field.

A good way of thinking about values is that as you strive towards your vision and goals, the values are there to make sure you don't do so at any cost.

Take the school list of values and elaborate on what they mean pragmatically for your programme, staff and students. Here are some examples:

- **Honesty** - we will be transparent in our dealings. We will communicate the reasoning behind big decisions. We will be honest in sports.
- **Respect** - we earn respect through acting upon our values and treating others with respect at all times. Especially on the sports-field. We are always respectful to each other, to other players, to the referees etc.
- **Self-Control** - we remain in control even when angered.
- **Equality** - we do not allow discrimination of any kind but work towards the support and inclusion for the whole community.
- **Care** - we care for our community and our environment. We are inclusive in activities. We always leave a place better than we found it.

The idea of this exercise is to clarify how your values apply pragmatically to the programme and everyone involved in it. Share your examples with coaches and leaders to illustrate how to use the school values in their sessions.

Coaches will be using the values as a tool on the sports field. Drama leaders will use them in their productions. Being part of the programme means being part of the culture, and the values frame your culture. Having some practical examples of the typical applications of your values helps your activity leaders understand how to use them.

As the framework of the values become more apparent for students and staff, it will make it easier for them to make good choices as they face difficult and complex situations. If your coaches and leaders undergo appraisals or reflections, reflecting on how values are talked about and applied practically during activity sessions will help ensure the transfer to students.

If you do not have values already defined by the school, then the following gives a short introduction on how to find the right ones for your programme.

How to Define Core Values

It is preferable to undergo a process to discover and uncover your values rather than pick them from a list. When we discover our values through a process, there is a higher chance of getting to the real core values rather than selecting what our intellectual mind thinks is "better" than the rest. However, it can be valuable to get a sense of what words are used to describe values. So, here are some examples:

<u>**Example List of Values**</u>

• Authenticity	• Friendships	• Poise
• Achievement	• Fun	• Popularity
• Adventure	• Growth	• Recognition
• Authority	• Happiness	• Religion
• Autonomy	• Honesty	• Reputation
• Balance	• Humour	• Respect
• Beauty	• Influence	• Responsibility
• Boldness	• Inner Harmony	• Security
• Compassion	• Justice	• Self-Respect
• Challenge	• Kindness	• Service
• Citizenship	• Knowledge	• Spirituality
• Community	• Leadership	• Stability
• Competency	• Learning	• Success
• Contribution	• Love	• Status
• Creativity	• Loyalty	• Trustworthiness
• Curiosity	• Meaningful Work	• Wealth
• Determination	• Openness	• Wisdom
• Fairness	• Optimism	
• Faith	• Peace	
• Fame	• Pleasure	

Scott Jeffry (7 Steps to Discovering Your Personal Core Values, 2014) suggests the following three processes of questioning to uncover your personal core values. They have been modified slightly to be applicable for ASP.

Peak Experiences

Consider an experience in the past where your programme was at its best. Perhaps an event that had everyone ecstatic and full of life. What was happening? What were you doing? What values were you fulfilling at that moment?

Suppressed Values

Think about a time when things were not going well, and people got upset or angry. Something rubbed them the wrong way. What was going on? What were the triggers? What were people feeling? Now, uncover what values were suppressed in that situation.

Code of Conduct

What do your students and staff need from the programme to experience the feeling of fulfilment? What value must be part of their life, if not, the programme risks being shallow?

Narrowing Down Your List of Values

We can uncover more than one value in each questioning process. After writing them all down, it is time to group them in related themes. Values like practice, application, doing, and application of knowledge are all related. Values like growth and development are also related. Select a word that represents the theme of each value group you have identified.

You may need to narrow down the list to the core values if you have amassed many. These questions may help reduce the list:

- What values are essential to the life of the programme?
- What values represent your ASP's primary way of operating?
- What values are essential to supporting the culture in your programme?

Around five values are usually enough to capture your programme's unique dimensions of being. Rank them in the order of importance.

Again, it is a good idea to take some time away and come back to work with a fresh mind. You might see things in a slightly different light and want to make some corrections.

5 DISCOVER PRESENT STATE

STRATEGIC PLANNING

Before plotting your course, you need to know where you are (i.e. determine your present state). By conducting audits (of documents, statistics and stakeholders), you can ascertain the current condition of your school and ASP. This information then lays the foundation for defining your focus areas, goals and projects later.

Mindmap of Audits

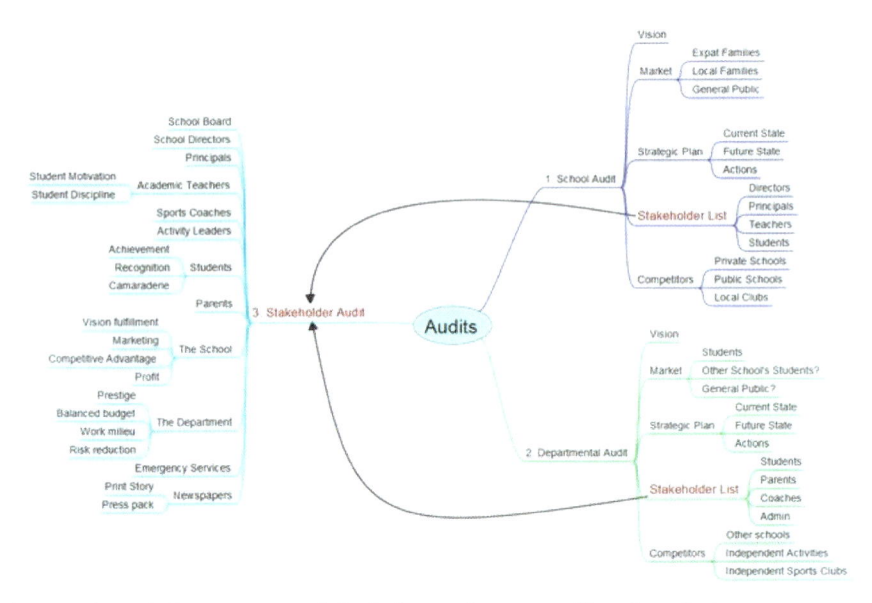

[Mindmap diagram showing Audits branching into three main categories:

1. School Audit — including Vision, Market (Expat Families, Local Families, General Public), Strategic Plan (Current State, Future State, Actions), Stakeholder List (Directors, Principals, Teachers, Students), Competitors (Private Schools, Public Schools, Local Clubs)

2. Departmental Audit — including Vision, Market (Students, Other School's Students?, General Public?), Strategic Plan (Current State, Future State, Actions), Stakeholder List (Students, Parents, Coaches, Admin), Competitors (Other schools, Independent Activities, Independent Sports Clubs)

3. Stakeholder Audit — including:
- *The School: School Board, School Directors, Principals, Academic Teachers (Student Motivation, Student Discipline), Sports Coaches, Activity Leaders, Students (Achievement, Recognition, Camaraderie), Parents*
- *The Department: Vision fulfillment, Marketing, Competitive Advantage, Profit, Prestige, Balanced budget, Work milieu, Risk reduction*
- *Newspapers: Emergency Services, Print Story, Press pack]*

As mentioned above, some of the information you will gather during your audits will be from documents (visions, plans, budgets, statistics) whilst the remainder will be collected from stakeholders using questionnaires and interviews.

Conducting audits is not a linear process; it is somewhat iterative and overlapping.

The auditing process often starts with a preliminary stakeholder analysis which tries to identify who the principal stakeholders are and how important each stakeholder is. We can organise the preliminary stakeholder analysis, as shown in the following table. Use the contact person field to identify a representative for the group so that you have contact details (no need to list all parents).

STRATEGIC PLANNING

Table of Stakeholders

Stakeholder Name	Contact Person Phone, email	Impact How much does the ASP impact them? (Low, Medium, High)	Influence How much influence do they have over the ASP?	What is important to the stakeholder? What is in it for them?	How could the stakeholder contribute?	How could the stakeholder block the ASP?	Strategy for engaging the stakeholder
Parent	Jane Doe Jane.doe@mail.com	Medium	Medium	Student progress, Cost, Social Networking, Security	Running the snack-bar, Chaperone, Volunteer	Voice any dissatisfaction within social network	Regular news on website, activity blog, invited to attend events
Local Newspaper	John Doe	Low	Medium	Getting a good story	Print stories about the school	Print negative stories	Develop press pack. Press meetings.

When considering the impact and influence of stakeholders, the following diagram can be useful. It compares the level of interest the stakeholder possesses against their power to help or hinder the programme.

Stakeholder Influence Diagram

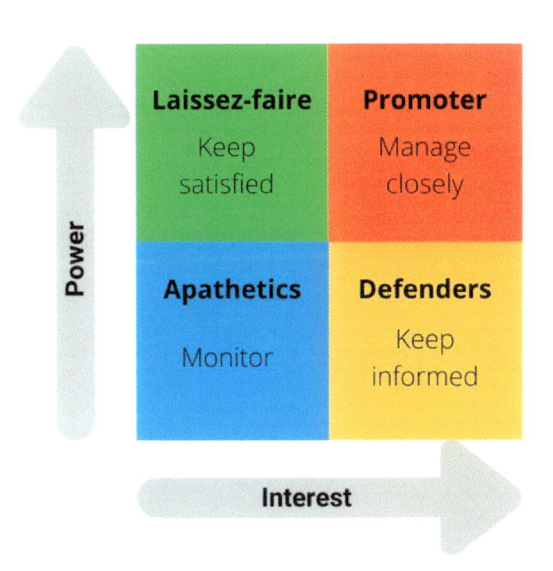

	Power ↑	
Laissez-faire Keep satisfied		**Promoter** Manage closely
Apathetics Monitor		**Defenders** Keep informed
	Interest →	

School Audit

As part of your school audit, consider who the school stakeholders are and if needed, update the preliminary stakeholder analysis you completed earlier. Consider what the various stakeholder's interests are, what is important to them and how they can hinder or help. Imagine each stakeholder asking the question "**What's in it for me?**".

Once the stakeholder analysis is updated, it is time to get personal with interviews and get information from surveys. Interview and survey questions typically fall under these areas:

- Personnel
- Quality
- Resources
- Benefits
- Processes
- Systems
- Culture
- Budget
- Support
- Procedures and policies

Leadership

It is valuable to spend some time and get the school leadership's view on what the strengths and weaknesses of your programme are. They have an intimate knowledge of the school strategy and are the decision-makers in areas that can affect your programme. Generally, they fall into your **promoter** group, and you should manage them closely. Meaning that you take their input seriously when considering what to put in your strategic plan.

Coaches and Activity Leaders

Use a mix between interviews and surveys to gain information from coaches and activity leaders. Focus your investigation on the present status of the programme and what staff want for the future.

Below are a few sample questions.

- Are you presently involved in some type of school extracurricular activity? If yes, please state which ones. If no, please state your reasons. What qualification do you have for that activity?
- Please rate your impression of the importance of the following activities. List of activities.
- Do you feel that these activities provide a wide enough variety? If no, please state preferred additions.
- Are there any school-based activities that would be best served by a community organisation? Please comment.
- Please check your level of agreement on how much benefit you feel extracurricular activities have on.
    - Students
    - School
    - Community
- Please indicate your level of agreement to the following statements.
    - Participating students are taught the values of good sportsmanship.
    - Participating students are taught the values of cooperation by being part of a team.
    - Participating students are given the opportunity to compete with their peers.
    - Students' interpersonal communication and social skills improve through extracurricular activities.
    - Students participation helps to prepare them for future adult leisure activities better.
    - Student participants who have been involved in extracurricular activities are more likely to assume leadership responsibilities in the community.
- Do you feel that you are adequately compensated for the work you do in extracurricular activities?
- In general, are coaches and activity leaders qualified to instruct extracurricular activities?
- Assuming the average season is 12 weeks long, how many hours do you think a coach of a significant activity contributes to the program in a season?
- Should all teachers be expected to participate in the extracurricular program? Reason.
- Are there any non-monetary benefits derived from involvement in an extracurricular activity? Please list the benefits.
- Are these benefits sufficient in themselves to merit involvement?
- Should teachers receive extra compensation for the time they assist

in the programme?

Continue to gather information from all school groups you have identified in your initial stakeholder analysis.

Stakeholder Audit

Use the information you have gathered and developed through the school audits to inform your decision on what information you want from your stakeholder audits.

Parents

This audit is about understanding the needs and wants of existing and future parents and students.

For information on future parents, the marketing department will be able to describe them as well as what their needs and wants are. It is valuable to interview a reliable person in marketing to get a clearer idea of what type of parents the school is targeting.

For existing parents and students, you can get information from the source. These information-gathering methods are useful:

- Creating a focus group
- Conducting individual interviews with high-value parents and students - high-value meaning families that stay with the school for years, have several children enrolled, are active in the activities and sports programme and talk positively about the programme.
- Conducting individual interviews with some new arrival parents to gain their impression.
- Sending out a general survey (excluding the families that have been interviewed so not to double up and overload them).
- Surveying parents whose children do not participate in activities may also be useful.

As you audit parents, focus on how the ASP is meeting their needs. The following bullet points represent, if met, the ideal relationship parents are looking for when dealing with an organisation (Alexander & Turner, 2001).

- Dealing with one person (or as few as possible) for the whole

programme experience.
- Telling the school information only once.
- Quickly obtain needed information at all interaction points.
- Recognition for who they are - their history and potential.
- Only receiving communication that is relevant to them.
- Flexibility to meet their individual requirements.

It is also useful to find out in what ways parents want to be involved and included within the ASP.

Students

The student audit should focus on the present perceived status of the programme as well as what students want for the future. The main focus areas tend to be on:

- **Variety** - does the programme offer enough variety of activities and are they of interest?
- **Quality** - do the activities teach the school values? Are there opportunities to compete? Are there opportunities to lead? Do communication skills improve? Do they feel safe? Etc.
- **Inclusivity** - can the students attend the activities they want? Do they feel part of an important group?
- **Celebration** - Do they feel recognised, valued and important?

Competitors

Your competitors are the ASPs in other schools. Their programmes will be similar but not the same as yours. It is useful to find out:

- How other ASPs have set up their programme.
- Which activities or sports they include and what their focus is.
- What sort of back-office systems are they using?
- Do they charge for their activities? If so, how much?
- Who leads their sports and activities? I.e. teachers, external coaches, external companies.
- Do they compensate their staff for running these activities? If so, how?

With this information, you can start to benchmark against other ASPs as well as find out how you will potentially differentiate your programme from theirs.

6 SWOT ANALYSIS

STRATEGIC PLANNING

SWOT stands for Strengths, Weaknesses, Opportunities and Threats. It is an excellent tool for establishing where you and your programme are right now. By assessing where you are, you can make the most of what you have, understand what your programme is lacking and where to improve and innovate.

Below are some topics worth considering when going through your strengths, weaknesses, opportunities and threats.

- **Personnel** - do you have the people you need, and are they well trained to deliver high-quality sessions? Are they motivated?
- **Resources** - what facilities and equipment do you have; is it optimally used?
- **Processes/Systems** - what processes and support systems do you have in place to make the programme run as efficiently and safely as possible?

  Example processes are:

  - Registration
  - Salary
  - Attendance
  - Communication
  - Event Management

  Sources of problems in a process are:

  - Staff have inadequate knowledge of how a process works.
  - Staff have inadequate knowledge of how a process **should** work.
  - People make errors and mistakes in executing procedures.
  - Current practises lack preventative measures.
  - The process includes unnecessary steps, inventory buffers, and wasteful measures.
  - There is a variation of inputs and outputs.

- **Culture** - how does the programme give opportunities and provide culture to the student body? Are they given responsibilities? Are there opportunities for students to give back?
- **Parents** - how does the programme give opportunities and provide culture to the parents? In what ways can parents be involved in the

programme?
- **Staff** - how does the programme give opportunities and provide culture to staff? How can staff be involved in the programme?
- **Budget and support** - do you have the resources you need? Is the school leadership supportive?
- **Procedures and policies** - are your procedures and policies set up to ensure the smooth and safe running of your programme? Do they provide the proper guidelines for the problems you face?
- **Collaboration** - does collaboration between activities, curriculum or even external agencies exist? For example, the Photography club takes pictures of sports events, and the news club writes about it.
- **Impressions** - what does the community as well as other schools think of your department and your ASP offerings now?

Strengths

Your strengths are what your programme (and the people in it) do exceptionally well. What distinguishes you from ASPs in other schools? What unique resources can you draw on? What do others see as your strengths?

Use the topics mentioned above to find what makes your programme work so well and what strengths you have that you can build on.

Weaknesses

Be honest! You must be realistic when considering the weaknesses of your programme. Think about what you can improve or innovate. What practices you should perhaps avoid. Where do you most often face problems? What are other people's opinions about the shortcomings of the programme? Consider your programme from the "customer's" point of view. Does everything run smoothly for them, or are there things that they may be less satisfied with?

Use the list given at the start to help uncover the program's weaknesses. It is crucial to find the root causes of any problem and verify with data before deciding on possible solutions and taking action.

Opportunities

Opportunities are openings or chances for something positive to happen. One possibility in Switzerland, for example, is to receive government funding for running sports activities with Jeunesse et Sport qualified coaches.

There may also be opportunities in the technologies you use. Is there a system available that will increase the efficiency of your department? Is there a club who is interested in a partnership?

Being able to spot and take advantage of opportunities can make a significant impact on your programme.

Threats

Threats include anything that can negatively affect the programme. An example of a "threat" that is facing many schools currently is the limitations put on ASPs to comply with government Coronavirus restrictions.

Another example could be that the school is planning to change its bus provider and have not evaluated or understood how this will affect your programme.

Yet another example of a "threat" might be a change of data management system that the school is using. The main point is to anticipate factors that could negatively affect your programme, allowing you to take mitigating action.

After you have finished the SWOT analysis, you will have a long list of possible actions to take. You will have a good idea of how to build on your strengths, take advantage of any identified opportunities, alleviate weaknesses and mitigate any threats.

7 DEFINE FOCUS AREAS

As you strive towards your vision, focus areas are the high-level areas you will be focusing your efforts on. At this level, there should still not be any particular metric or deadline. The idea of focus areas is to define what matters for your programme moving into the future.

Use your findings from the SWOT analysis to help uncover the focus areas you want for your strategic plan. Your focus areas should be specific enough to channel your goals and projects towards achieving your vision.

The rule is, if a project or improvement does not fit into one of your focus areas - it should not be happening - at least not right now. Sure there may be exceptions to the rule. However, keep in mind that you have limited resources to move your ASP towards your vision.

Around three to six focus areas are a reasonable range. Here are some rules of thumb for creating focus areas.

- **Keep it short** - it needs to be simple, focused and memorable. No longer than six words.
- **Keep it narrow** - you need to be able to identify specific goals and projects that fall under your focus areas.
- **State the outcome** - avoid words like "maximise" or "succeed". State the result you want to achieve, not how you are going to do it.
- **No metrics** - metrics play a significant role in your planning but not at this stage. Keep things high level, but still, outcome-focused.

Often the focus areas fit into one of the following broad categories:

- **Expansion/Growth** - e.g. expanding the programme, often coupled with the development of the school and the intake of more students.
- **Budget/ Cost** - e.g. here are cuts in the budget, or more money is needed to make things work.
- **Student and Parent Satisfaction** - e.g. making sure the programme is meeting the needs of the students and the families.
- **Compliance** - e.g. compliance with law, rules or regulation.
- **Innovation** - e.g. adding new strands of activities or sports.
- **Engagement** - e.g. engaging with our community.
- **Employee Happiness** - e.g. Proud and happy coaches and leaders.

The categories mentioned above are by no means the full list, but hopefully, they give you a starting point for creating your focus areas.

STRATEGIC PLANNING

Remember that your overall objective when designing the focus areas is to realise your vision statement.

Here are some focus area examples:

- Parent Engagement
- Student Leadership
- Clear Communication
- Qualified Coaches and Leaders
- Programme Assessment

Ask yourself, if I succeed with these focus areas, are they taking me towards my vision? If you find that your focus areas are not taking you towards your vision, then you either need to revisit your focus areas or revisit your vision statement.

It is also worth looking at how your focus areas align with your values. The values help set the culture in your programme, and the culture is what enables staff, students, to carry out their activities in line with the vision. Not every focus area has to align with a value, but it is good to draw the connection if they do.

E.g. the value, **Continuous Learning** connects with the focus areas **Student Leadership** and **Qualified Coaches and Leaders**.

8 STRATEGIC GOALS AND PROJECTS

Through the audits and SWOT analysis, you have defined your present state. Your ASP vision and focus areas give you direction towards your future state. Now, it is time to more specifically define your desired future state in terms of goals and then conduct a gap analysis to bridge the gap between your present and future state.

Steps Towards Defining Goals and Projects

Determine your current state → Detfine your desired state → Conduct a gap analysis → Prioritize your actionable items → Find the best sequence

When deciding on your goals, balance being ambitious about developing the programme with being realistic in terms of day-to-day priorities and ensuring that you have actions to bridge the two.

While defining your goals, consider how the following points constrain your goals:

- Budget
- Time
- Policies
- Infrastructure
- Technological Infrastructure
- Resources
- Culture

Remember to set realistic and achievable goals. It is much more motivating for you and your staff when you go on to achieve your goals rather than be at 50% when a deadline arrives.

Strategic Goals

Strategic goals are the heart and soul of your plan. They state what you want to achieve, are aligned to one or more of your focus areas and have a deadline attached to them. Typically, between 3-6 goals per focus area are enough.

Once you achieve a goal, replace it with another one. A good way of thinking about your strategic goals is: If you are meeting with the school leadership, what would be the key goals of your programme that you would update them on?

Keep your goals about one sentence long. You need to be able, to sum up, what you want to achieve quickly and simply.

It is helpful to use the following structure:

Detail + Action + Deadline

E.g.

- ASP handbook updated by 30 October 2021
- Parent satisfaction score of 70% achieved by 2 May 2022
- All coaches have completed the positive coaching course by 27 August 2021

Remember that these goals need to be stated as goals and not as statements of intent. Each strategic goal will have projects linked underneath it that will detail what will be done to achieve it.

Present State Goals

These are the day-to-day goals associated with running your ASP. What needs to be done right now for the programme to be successful? Usually, these goals are about improving performance and existing processes.

Example:

- The ASP handbook is updated by 20 August 2021

Future State Goals

Future state goals are things that take a lot of time and effort to bring into place. They may need research and pilot programmes before they can be fully implemented. These are goals that introduce new elements to your ASP.

Some examples are:

- LTAD framework has been adapted and implemented into the ASP by 1 September 2023
- Custom IT systems for attendance, competitions, ASP registrations and salaries implemented by 1 September 2023
- 70% of all sports activities are qualified and registered for J+S funding by 15 October 2023.

Bridging Goals

Take your future state goals and work backwards towards present state goals. What do you need to do to go from where you are now to where you want to be? Bridging goals often include research projects, piloting phase and development goals.

Example:

The competition module pilot completed by 7 December 2021

Projects

Your projects describe what you will do to achieve your goals. The purpose of your projects is to effect and manage change from a current state to a desired future state.

Start by considering one of your present state goals. Uncover what exactly you need to do to achieve the goal. List the actionable items and organise them into manageable projects. There can be several projects linked to a goal or just one.

Steps Towards Defining Goals and Projects

Determine your current state → Define your desired state → Conduct a gap analysis → Prioritize your actionable items → Find the best sequence

Simple Gap Analysis Table

Gap Analysis	Current State (FROM)	Future State (TO)	GAPS	Actions
Item 1				
Item 2				
Item 3				
Item 4				

Depending on how complex your project is, there are two main ways to set them up. The first is creating a single project with multiple tasks attached. Tasks are either completed or not completed. You don't have 30% progress. It is either yes or no. Your projects, however, have stages of completion that are represented by its tasks. A project can be 30% completed. It is helpful to write it up in Gantt format, as shown in the project overview excel example.

STRATEGIC PLANNING

Project Overview Excel Example

PROJECT TITLE				
	Project Start:	Tue, 1/1/2019		
[Project Lead]	Today:	Wed, 1/9/2019		
	Display Week:	1		

TASK	ASSIGNED TO	START	END
Phase 1 Title			
Task 1		1/1/19	1/4/19
Task 2		1/5/19	1/7/19
Task 3		1/8/19	1/12/19
Task 4		1/13/19	1/18/19
Task 5		1/6/19	1/8/19
Phase 2 Title			
Task 1		1/7/19	1/11/19
Task 2		1/9/19	1/14/19
Task 3		1/15/19	1/18/19
Task 4		1/15/19	1/17/19

There may be times when you need a larger, more complex project. Then you will have to break it into sub-projects sitting underneath your main project. Otherwise, you risk ending up with a list of tasks that are difficult to manage. So, if a project is complex, further breaking it down into sub-projects is a valuable method to make the project more manageable.

9 MONITOR PROGRESS

The completion of projects related to your strategic goals goes a long way in measuring your success in moving towards your vision. However, it is also necessary to keep a finger on the pulse of your ASP in general. It is essential to know whether or not you are delivering value, and if there is any movement, you should be aware of, i.e. participation decreasing or costs going up. Therefore, some degree of measurement is needed.

To this end, it is necessary to define general areas of your ASP suitable for monitoring the programme's health. You must define key metrics, often called Key Performance Indicators (KPIs) which by their value, give a measure of your ASP's overall health.

KPI's should focus on:

- **Measures for customer excellence** - i.e. being excellent in the eyes of the students and parents.
- **Internal measures for excellence** - demonstrating the value you are delivering to the school and its leadership.

You need to find the targets that make sense to measure for your ASP. Following are some commonly used ones:

- **Parent satisfaction** - survey results on communication, organisation etc.
- **Student satisfaction** - survey results on quality of activities, relationships with staff and other components.
- **Staff satisfaction** - survey results on support, adequate systems adequate, equipment etc.
- **Cost per student** - this could be per activity or across the ASP.
- **Percentage cost per area** - i.e. competitive sports, art, Science Technology Engineering Math (STEM). It is useful for measuring the size of one area and comparing it to another.
- **Percentage participation per area** - the percentage of students signed up for each area (competitive sport, recreational sport, art etc.). Is there an area that needs more attention?
- **Staff to administration ratio** - meaning, how many coaches and leaders is your department managing? If this ratio is too low, say two administrators for 50 staff, it may be hard for admin to be on top of scheduling, organisation, finances etc.
- **The number of student signups vs accepted** - this metric will help you understand which activities are popular and support your decision making on capacity.

- **Percentage of staff with certificates** - e.g. coaching certificates or first aid certificate etc. Do they a need refresher first aid course?
- **The number of staff training sessions per year** - ensuring staff are in touch with the latest teaching, coaching and programme knowledge to ensure students receive the best education.
- **Staff attendance rates** - are staff meeting up to their scheduled sessions? Low attendance rates hurt the programme.
- **Student attendance rates** - are students committed to the ASP?
- **Staff retention rate** - how many leaders and coaches stay on?
- **Age of facilities and equipment** - when do things need to be updated or replaced?
- **Number of safety inspections** - equipment checks.
- **Social media engagement** - this can show you the community engagement with the content and events your ASP is producing.
- **The number of complaints** - this becomes useful if you compare against previous years and to discover patterns.

Governance

It is vital to have at least some form of governance related to your strategic plan. How else will you keep on top of your strategy and progress? Following are some commonly used governance elements:

- **Goals reporting** - commit to reporting to the school leadership team or your line manager about your progress related to your strategic goals. Set a frequency that works for you.
- **Project updates** - these are ad hoc updates to you from responsible staff on progress and challenges related to the active projects.
- **KPI measurements** - set a frequency for measuring your KPIs.
- **End of year report** - create an end of year report that analyses the progress made, challenges, changes and health of the ASP.

10 SUMMARY

STRATEGIC PLANNING

There are six stages you should follow when creating your ASP strategic plan;

1. Preparation
2. Creating your vision
3. Discovering your present state
4. Defining your focus areas
5. Defining your strategic goals and related projects
6. Monitor your progress

In the **preparation** stage, you focus on acquiring fundamental knowledge and gaining support.

Creating your vision is about aligning your ASPs ideal future with the school's overall vision.

Discovering your present state is about auditing the ASP stakeholders and understanding your ASP's strengths and weaknesses.

Defining your focus areas is where you decide what matters for your programme.

Defining your strategic goals and related projects is the crux of the planning and helps you detail which actions to take and when.

In the final stage, **monitor your progress,** you define what to measure and how to govern the progress of your goals and actionable items.

STRATEGIC PLANNING

REFEFENCES

7 Steps to Discovering Your Personal Core Values. (2014, June 4). Scott Jeffrey. https://scottjeffrey.com/personal-core-values/https://www.ymcarichmond.org/about-us-ymca/mission-vision/

About Us | International School of Lausanne, Switzerland. (2020). International School of Lausanne. https://www.isl.ch/about-us/

Alexander, D., & Turner, C. (2001). The C.R.M. Pocketbook.

Catalano, R. F., Berglund, M. L., Ryan, J. A. M., Lonczak, H. S., & Hawkins, J. D. (2004). Positive Youth Development in the United States: Research Findings on Evaluations of Positive Youth Development Programs. The Annals of the American Academy of Political and Social Science, 591, 98–124.

Csikszentmihalyi, M., Rathunde, K., & Whalen, S. (1993). Talented Teenagers:
The Roots of Success and Failure. In British Journal of Educational Studies—BRIT J EDUC STUD (Vol. 42). https://doi.org/10.2307/3121889

Eccles, J. S., Barber, B. L., & Hunt, J. (2003). Extracurricular activities and adolescent development. Journal of Social Issues, 59(4), 865–889.

Lamothe, G. (2013, September 13). *Why is Strategy Important?* https://www.mnp.ca/en/Posts-Site/Pages/Why-is-Strategy-Important.aspx

Larson, R. (2000). Toward a Psychology of Positive Youth Development. The American Psychologist, 55, 170–183. https://doi.org/10.1037//0003-066X.55.1.170

Mahoney, J. L. (2000). Student extracurricular activity participation as a Moderator in the development of antisocial patterns. Child Development, 71(2).

Nike. (2020). Nike's Mission Statement. Nike News. https://about.nike.com/

Petitpas, A., Cornelius, A., Vanraalte, J., & Jones, T. (2005). A Framework for Planning Youth Sport Programs That Foster Psychosocial Development. The Sport Psychologist, 19, 63–80. https://doi.org/10.1123/tsp.19.1.63

Wikipedia. (2020). Strategy. In Wikipedia. https://en.wikipedia.org/w/index.php?title=Strategy&oldid=988329699

YMCA. (2020). Mission & Vision. YMCA of Greater Richmond. https://www.ymcarichmond.org/about-us-ymca/mission-vision/

GOT FEEDBACK?

Got feedback about the content of this booklet? I would love hearing from you! Send me an email to EDOTAC@gmail.com with the title of the booklet in the subject line and share your thoughts.

ABOUT THE AUTHOR

As Director of Athletics and Activities, Erlend Badham, has successfully led strategic development and change of Activities and Sports Porgrammes in several international schools.

Printed in Great Britain
by Amazon